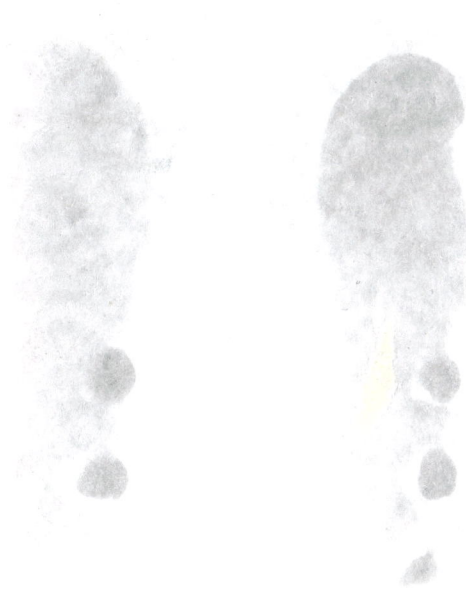

RAINTREE BIOGRAPHIES

Crazy Horse

D.L. Birchfield

RAINTREE
Steck-Vaughn
PUBLISHERS

A Harcourt Company

Austin   New York
www.raintreesteckvaughn.com

Copyright © 2003 Steck-Vaughn Company

All rights reserved. No part of this book may be reproduced or utilized in any form or by any means, electronic or mechanical, including photocopying, recording, or by any information storage and retrieval system, without permission in writing from the Publisher. Inquiries should be addressed to: Copyright Permissions, Steck-Vaughn Company, P.O. Box 26015, Austin, TX 78755.

Published by Raintree Steck-Vaughn Publishers, an imprint of Steck-Vaughn Company.

Project Editors: Sean Dolan, Gianna Williams
Production Manager: Richard Johnson
Designed by Ian Winton

Planned and produced by Discovery Books

Library of Congress Cataloging-in-Publication Data
Available upon request

ISBN 0-7398-5673-1

Printed and bound in China
1 2 3 4 5 6 7 8 9 0 07 06 05 04 03 02

Acknowledgments
The publishers would like to thank the following for permission to reproduce their pictures:
Cover: Peter Newark's Western Americana; p. 4 Peter Newark's Western Americana; p. 5 Bridgeman Art Library; p. 6 Peter Newark's American Pictures; p. 7 Bridgeman Art Library; p. 8 Peter Newark's Western Americana; p. 9 Peter Newark's American Pictures; p. 10 Mary Evans Picture Library; p. 11 Bridgeman Art Library; pp. 12 & 13 Peter Newark's Western Americana; pp. 14 & 15 Peter Newark's American Pictures; p. 16 Peter Newark's Western Americana; p. 17 Peter Newark's American Pictures; p. 18 Peter Newark's Western Americana; p. 19 Peter Newark's American Pictures; p. 21 Peter Newark's Military Pictures; p. 22 Peter Newark's American Pictures; pp. 23 & 24 Peter Newark's Western Americana; pp. 25 & 26 Corbis; p. 27 Bridgeman Art Library; pp. 28 & 29 Corbis.

Maps by Stefan Chabluk.

Contents

A Famous Battle   4
A Child of the Plains   6
War Comes to the Lakotas   8
Vision Quest   10
Gold Brings Trouble   12
The Lakotas Win a War   14
A "Shirt-Wearer"   16
Preparing to Fight   18
The Battle of the Rosebud   20
Custer's Last Stand   22
Defeat and Surrender   24
The Man Who Died Fighting   26
The Man Remembered   28
Timeline   30
Glossary   31
Further Reading and Information   31
Index   32

A Famous Battle

On the afternoon of June 25, 1876, a man named Crazy Horse was in his tepee, in a large encampment of Lakota and Cheyenne people on the banks of the Little Bighorn River, in present-day southern Montana. The encampment stretched out for almost 4 miles, and was home to 7,000 people. Almost 2,000 of those people were warriors. Of these, none was more respected than Crazy Horse.

For a time, some people thought this was a photo of Crazy Horse, but the great Lakota warrior never let his picture be taken.

A Modest Appearance

"Crazy Horse was a man not very tall and not very short, neither broad nor thin. His hair was very light....Crazy Horse had a very light complexion....His face was not broad, and he had a high, sharp nose. He had black eyes that hardly ever looked straight at a man, but they didn't miss much that was going on, all the same...."

Short Buffalo (Oglala Lakota), interview with Eleanor Hinman, July 13, 1930

Word reached Crazy Horse that soldiers were attacking the north end of the encampment. These were the men of the U.S. 7th Cavalry, under the command of Lieutenant Colonel George Armstrong Custer.

In this painting, an Indian artist, Kills Two, depicts Crazy Horse in battle with Custer. Kills Two was born in 1869 and would have been about 7 years old when the Battle of the Little Bighorn took place.

Crazy Horse gathered warriors behind him and led them across the river, into one of the most famous battles of all time. "Custer's Last Stand," also known as the Battle of the Little Bighorn, or the Battle of the Greasy Grass, was the greatest, and the last, of the Native American victories in the Indian wars of the American West.

A Child of the Plains

Crazy Horse was born about 1838, near the Black Hills of present-day western South Dakota. His people were the Oglala, one of many different groups that made up the Lakota tribe. The Lakotas depended upon the buffalo for their way of life. There were millions of buffalo on the upper Great Plains where they lived. They provided meat for food, hides for tepees and clothing, sinews for bow strings and sewing thread, and rawhide for shields and ropes.

The American artist George Catlin painted this scene of Plains Indians hunting buffalo in about 1835. Catlin traveled throughout the West and made many paintings of Native Americans. Crazy Horse was a skilled horseman even at a young age.

Lakotas

The Lakotas are one of the three main divisions of the Sioux people: Lakotas (Teton), Nakotas (Yankton), and Dakotas (Santee). The Lakotas are divided into seven subtribes: Oglala, Sincongu, Miniconju, Hunkpapa, Oohenonpa, Itazipco, and Sihasapa. Crazy Horse's father was an Oglala, and his mother was a Sincongu Lakota.

Crazy Horse's father was a medicine man whose name was also Crazy Horse. His mother was called Rattle Blanket Woman. Lakotas take different names at different times in their lives. As a young boy, Crazy Horse was called Curly Hair or Light Hair, but the first name he earned was His-Horse-On-Sight, because of his ability to catch wild horses and tame them, and his skill at stealing horses from other tribes.

These Sioux moccasins date from about 1890. They are made of buckskin, rawhide, fabric, and glass beads.

As a teenager, Crazy Horse often rode off alone to spend days by himself in the wilderness. This alarmed the tribal elders. But Crazy Horse loved to be alone, and he would prefer his own company to being with other people for the rest of his life.

WAR COMES TO THE LAKOTAS

In 1854, when Crazy Horse was a teenager, a terrible misunderstanding led to the death of many people.

It began when a cow wandered away from a wagon train on the Oregon Trail and into a village of his mother's people, the Sincongu Lakotas. A visiting Miniconju Lakota man shot the cow. The owner of the cow complained to the U.S. Army, and Lieutenant John Grattan led 28 soldiers to arrest the man who shot the cow.

THE OREGON TRAIL

The Oregon trail ran from Independence, Missouri, to the Columbia River region of Oregon. Along the way, it passed along the southern edge of Lakota country, along the Platte River in Nebraska. By the 1850s, more than 50,000 Americans were traveling on the trail each year to reach the Pacific Northwest. Those travelers depleted the buffalo in that area and caused conflict with the Indians along the trail.

A Sioux camp on the Great Plains. It was painted by Karl Bodmer in 1833. Crazy Horse would have grown up in a camp like this one.

The Miniconju man refused to be arrested, and the village chief, Conquering Bear, tried to explain that a Sincongu chief had no authority to make a Miniconju man surrender. In response, Grattan ordered his artillery to fire on the village. Among those killed was Conquering Bear. The villagers then attacked and killed all the soldiers.

A year later, to punish the Lakotas, the army attacked and destroyed a different Lakota village on Bluewater Creek. About 90 Sincongu people were killed, and many others were taken prisoner. These terrible events had a lasting effect on the Lakota people.

Vision Quest

Not long after the tragedy at Bluewater Creek, Crazy Horse went on a vision quest. Young Lakotas sought a vision to help guide them in life. They purified themselves by ceremonies and then fasted for several days alone to seek a vision. Elders would help them interpret their vision.

George Catlin's painting of a Sioux Sun Dance. The Sun Dance is a summer ceremony of the Sioux and other Northern Plains Indians.

A Quiet Man

"[Crazy Horse] never spoke in council and attended very few. There was no special reason for this, it was just his nature. He was a very quiet man except when there was fighting."

He Dog (Oglala Lakota), interview with Eleanor Hinman, July 7, 1930

Characteristically, Crazy Horse did not perform the usual purification rituals before going on his vision quest. Throughout his life, he rarely participated in tribal ceremonies or councils.

Paha Sapa

To the Lakotas, the Black Hills are sacred land. They call them Paha Sapa, "the heart of everything that is." Crazy Horse would become famous for fighting to protect Paha Sapa from intrusion by the United States. Today, the Lakotas are still seeking to reclaim Paha Sapa through the U.S. legal system.

Instead, without telling anyone, he rode out alone into the prairies near the Black Hills. There, he fasted and prayed. After a couple of days he had a vision of a warrior in battle, floating above the ground on a horse. The horseman told Crazy Horse to be humble and dress plainly and not to keep anything for himself. He was to devote his life to protecting and feeding his people.

GOLD BRINGS TROUBLE

Not long after his vision quest, Crazy Horse earned the name that he is remembered by. On a raid against the Arapahos, he displayed daring and bravery and killed two enemy warriors when they rode out to challenge him. His father now gave his own name to his son.

As Crazy Horse gained fame among his people by his daring raids against enemy tribes, a gold strike at Bozeman, Montana, soon brought trouble to the Lakotas. The U.S. Army opened a trail to Bozeman, right through the heart of Oglala territory in eastern Wyoming and southern Montana. They built three forts on the Bozeman Trial to protect it: Fort Phil Kearny and Fort Reno in Wyoming, and Fort C.F. Smith in Montana.

A painting of Crazy Horse by Robert Lindneux. In keeping true to his vision, Crazy Horse always dressed much more plainly than he is depicted here.

From 1865 to 1867 Crazy Horse followed the Oglala leader, Red Cloud, into war with the U.S. Army. In the war over the Bozeman Trail, Crazy Horse gained fame as a brilliant military leader. It was the most successful Native American war against the U.S. government.

Red Cloud led the Lakotas in the war over the Bozeman Trail.

INTERVIEWS WITH INDIANS

Most of what is known about Crazy Horse's life comes from interviews with Oglalas and other people who knew him. Judge E. S. Ricker conducted many of those interviews in 1906–1907. In 1930–1931, Mari Sandoz and Eleanor Hinman conducted more interviews. The interviews are preserved in the Nebraska State Historical Society library.

The Lakotas Win a War

On December 21, 1866, Captain William Fetterman and 80 men were patrolling the trails near Fort Phil Kearny. Crazy Horse allowed the soldiers to see him, and lured them into chasing him further and further away from the fort. Finally, the soldiers chased him over a hill, where hundreds of Lakota warriors were hiding. Fetterman and all his men were killed.

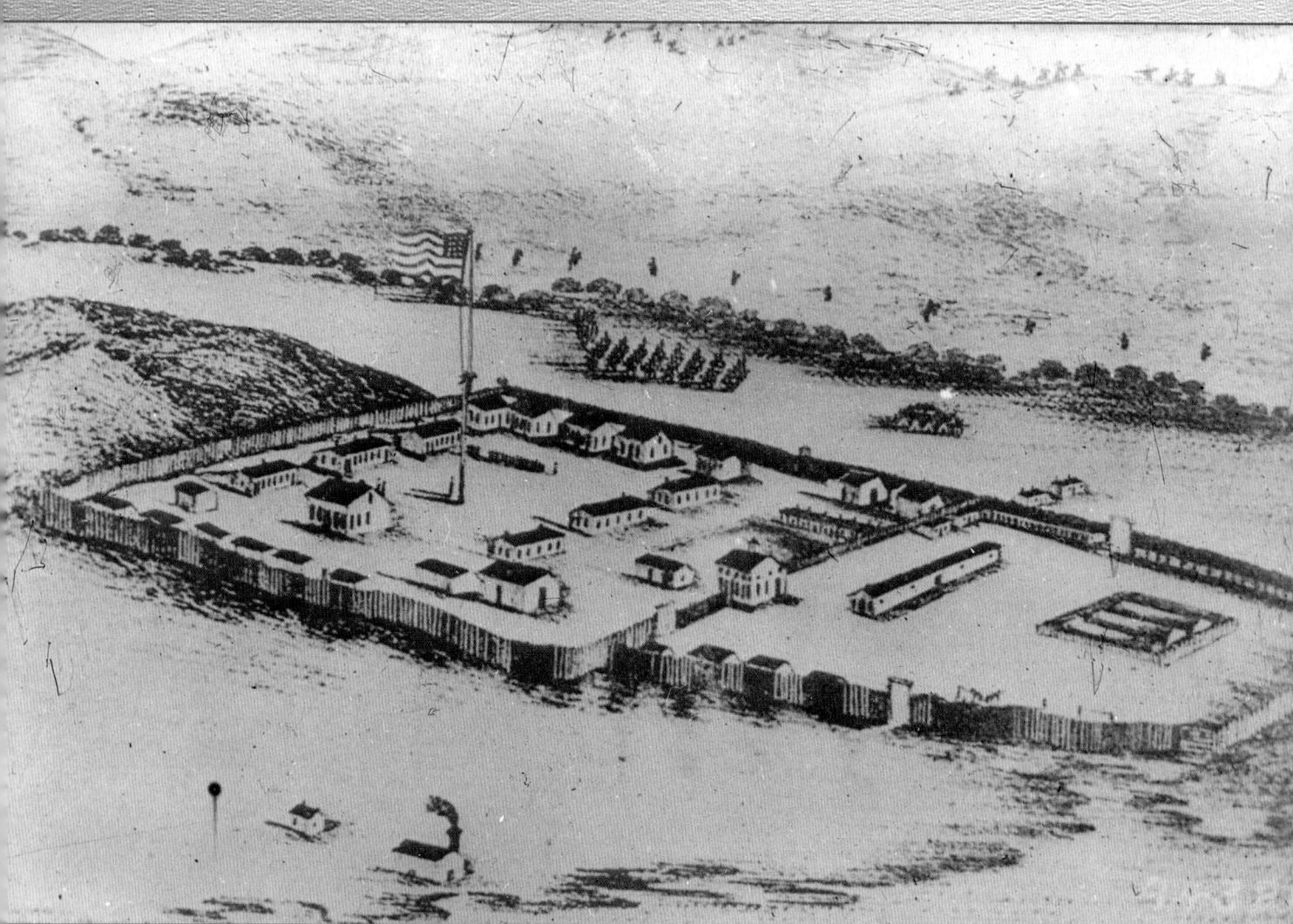

Fort Phil Kearny on the Bozeman Trail was burned by the Lakotas after it was abandoned by the U.S. Army in 1868.

Alexander Gardner's photo of the negotiations at the Treaty of Fort Laramie in April 1868. Red Cloud and other Sioux leaders are meeting with the highest ranking army officer, General William Tecumseh Sherman, and the U.S. treaty commissioners.

A Man of Strategy

"[Crazy Horse] didn't like to start a battle unless he had it all planned out in his head and knew he was going to win. He always used judgment and played safe. His brother and High Back Bone were reckless. That is why they got killed."

He Dog (Oglala Lakota), interview with Eleanor Hinman, July 7, 1930

After Red Cloud won several more victories, the army abandoned the Bozeman Trail. By the terms of the Treaty of Fort Laramie in 1868, the United States conceded all of present-day South Dakota west of the Missouri River to the Oglalas forever. This land included the sacred Black Hills. The three isolated forts were abandoned.

A "Shirt-Wearer"

In 1869, the transcontinental railroad was finished. The east and west coasts of the United States were now connected by rail. The railroad brought large numbers of professional buffalo hunters to the Great Plains. In a short time, they destroyed the buffalo herds on which the Lakotas and other Native Americans depended.

A Currier and Ives print from 1868. The railroads were seen as bringing "civilization" to the "wild, untamed" West.

By that time, Crazy Horse had won one of the highest honors of his people, that of Shirt-Wearer. It was a position of respect that required him to be an example to others and look out for the welfare of the poor among the Lakota.

He lost that honor because of a human weakness. He fell in love with Black Buffalo Woman, who was the wife of another man, named No Water. The two lovers ran away together, but No Water followed them and shot Crazy Horse in the jaw with a pistol.

THE BUFFALO HERDS

A single buffalo can weigh 2,000 pounds and stand 6 feet tall. The number of buffalo on the Great Plains in 1850 has been estimated at 75 million. The animals were almost exterminated in the 1870s by commercial buffalo hunters, who sold their hides for about one dollar each. By 1884, there were only about 300 buffalo left on the Great Plains.

The incident nearly caused a war among the Oglala people. Great diplomacy was required to prevent violence, and Crazy Horse lost his status of Shirt-Wearer. Some Lakotas saw Crazy Horse as a troublemaker after that. Even so, he was still repected as a warrior.

Preparing to Fight

Despite the Treaty of Fort Laramie, white prospectors were soon trespassing in the Black Hills in search of gold. In 1874, Lieutenant Colonel George Custer led a U.S. Army expedition into the Black Hills.

Soon Custer sent reports that the Black Hills were filled with gold "from the grass roots down." A wild gold rush followed, with thousands of prospectors pouring into the sacred land of the Lakotas.

George Armstrong Custer, photographed by Mathew Brady. Custer first became famous as a calvary officer in the Civil War.

The U.S. government ordered all Lakotas (and other tribes in the area) onto reservations. The government also tried to buy the Black Hills. Two large groups of Lakotas, led by Crazy Horse and the medicine man Sitting Bull, refused to go to the reservations.

The gold rush town of Deadwood, in the Black Hills, about 1877. The gold rush brought thousands of miners into the Lakotas' sacred land.

On January 7, 1876, the government declared all Indians who had not come into reservations to be hostile. Shortly after, the U.S. government sent the Army to bring Crazy Horse and Sitting Bull in.

Earning Respect

"All Indians gave [Crazy Horse] a high reputation for courage and generosity. In advancing upon an enemy, none of his warriors were allowed to pass him. He had made himself hundreds of friends by his charity toward the poor, as it was a point of honor with him never to keep anything for himself, excepting weapons of war. I never heard an Indian mention his name save in terms of respect."

Captain John G. Bourke, U.S. Army, *On the Border with Crook*

The Battle of the Rosebud

In the spring of 1876, thousands of Lakotas gathered in a large encampment with their Cheyenne allies in a valley along the Little Bighorn River in southern Montana, known to Lakotas as the Greasy Grass River.

Many of the important events and places in Crazy Horse's life took place on or near the Bozeman Trail.

When they learned that a large U.S. Army of about 1,000 soldiers was marching toward them from the south to destroy their camp, about 1,000 Native Americans, led by Crazy Horse, rode out to try to stop the enemy.

General George Crook was the commanding officer of the U.S. Army forces at the Battle of the Rosebud.

On June 17, 1876, about 30 miles from their camp, the Native Americans found General George Crook's army on Rosebud Creek. The Battle of the Rosebud lasted all day. When the fighting was over, Crook's army had been defeated. His forces withdrew to his base camp, unable to reinforce troops led by Custer, who was nearing the encampment on the Little Bighorn.

Good Judgment

"In the Rosebud fight the soldiers first got the Sioux and Cheyenne on the run. Crazy Horse, Bad Heart Bull, Black Deer, Kicking Bear, and Good Weasel rallied the Sioux, turned the charge, and got the soldiers on the run....When these five commenced to rally their men, that was as far as the soldiers got. Crook moved back to Goose Creek after the fight....Crazy Horse used good judgment in this Rosebud fight."

Short Buffalo, interview with Eleanor Hinman, July 13, 1930

Custer's Last Stand

Eight days after the Battle of the Rosebud, an advance column of cavalry, led by Custer, arrived near the huge Indian encampment on June 25, 1876. Custer was the most aggressive officer in the United States Army. Wherever he found the enemy, he always attacked.

In 1881, an Indian artist, Red Horse, made this painting of the Battle of the Little Bighorn. The battle is known to the Lakota as the Battle of the Greasy Grass.

The First Man to Cross the River

"Crazy Horse rode up… [and said] 'There's a good fight coming over the hill.' I looked where he pointed and saw Custer and his bluecoats pouring over the hill. I thought there were a million of them…. [Crazy Horse] was not a bit excited. He made a joke of it…. He was the first man to cross the river…."

Short Buffalo (Oglala Lakota), interview with Eleanor Hinman, July 13, 1930

"Custer's Last Stand," painted by Edgar S. Paxson. The battle is the most famous in the history of the West.

Crow Indian scouts tried to warn Custer that he was greatly outnumbered. They told him that if he advanced "we will all go home by a road we do not know." But Custer ignored the warnings. Instead he divided his forces into three groups. One group never reached the camp. The other, led by Miles Reno, attacked the north end of the village and was easily driven away.

After driving off Reno's men, the Indian leaders Crazy Horse, Sitting Bull, Hump, Two Moon, and Gall caught Custer and his 240 men in the open. With more than 1,000 Cheyenne and Lakota warriors surrounding them, Custer and all the men riding with him were killed within a short time.

Defeat and Surrender

After their victory over Custer, the Indians made no serious attempt to attack the other two groups. The day after the battle, the Indians scattered in different directions to hunt buffalo. Outraged at Custer's defeat, the U.S. Army pursued the Lakotas and Cheyennes relentlessly, until only Sitting Bull and Crazy Horse and their people remained free.

The Lakota medicine man Sitting Bull was photographed by T. G. Anderton in 1878 at Fort Walsh, Canada. Sitting Bull was killed while resisting a U.S. government attempt to have him arrested in 1890.

Sitting Bull led his Hunkpapa Lakota people to the temporary safety of Canada, but Crazy Horse tried to survive the winter with his Oglala people in the Powder River country of Wyoming and Montana.

The winter of 1876–1877 was particularly cold. There were few buffalo left on the plains, and the cold and snow made it hard for the Lakotas to hunt. By the spring of 1877, Crazy Horse's people were starving. On May 6, 1877, Crazy Horse negotiated a surrender, along with more than 900 of his people.

A few miles from Fort Robinson, Nebraska, was where Crazy Horse was ordered to camp after he surrendered.

The Surrender

"On a big flat near Fort Robinson, Red Cloud and White Hat (Lieutenant Clark) and two troops of cavalry met Crazy Horse. They shook hands and said they were glad to see him; everybody had come in peace. Crazy Horse spread out his blanket for Red Cloud to sit on and gave his shirt to Red Cloud; He Dog did the same for White Hat. This meant that they gave up to these two...."

Short Buffalo (Oglala Lakota), interview with Eleanor Hinman, July 13, 1930

A Man Who Died Fighting

Once Crazy Horse surrendered, he was required to remain camped within a few miles of Fort Robinson, in western Nebraska. He had been promised that his people would be given their own reservation, and that they would be allowed to go on a buffalo hunt.

Throughout the summer of 1877, Crazy Horse tried to get the Army to keep its promises. When the Army resisted, Crazy Horse grew restless. Afraid that Crazy Horse might lead his people away from Fort Robinson, the head of the War Department, General William Tecumseh Sherman, ordered that Crazy Horse be arrested. The plan was then to imprison him on an island off the coast of Florida.

General William Tecumseh Sherman as he appeared as a Union general during the Civil War.

Crazy Horse was only told that the commander of Fort Robinson wanted to talk to him. Once inside the fort, when he saw that he was being taken to a cell, Crazy Horse tried to get away. As several soldiers held him, another stabbed him with a bayonet. Crazy Horse died that night, on September 5, 1877.

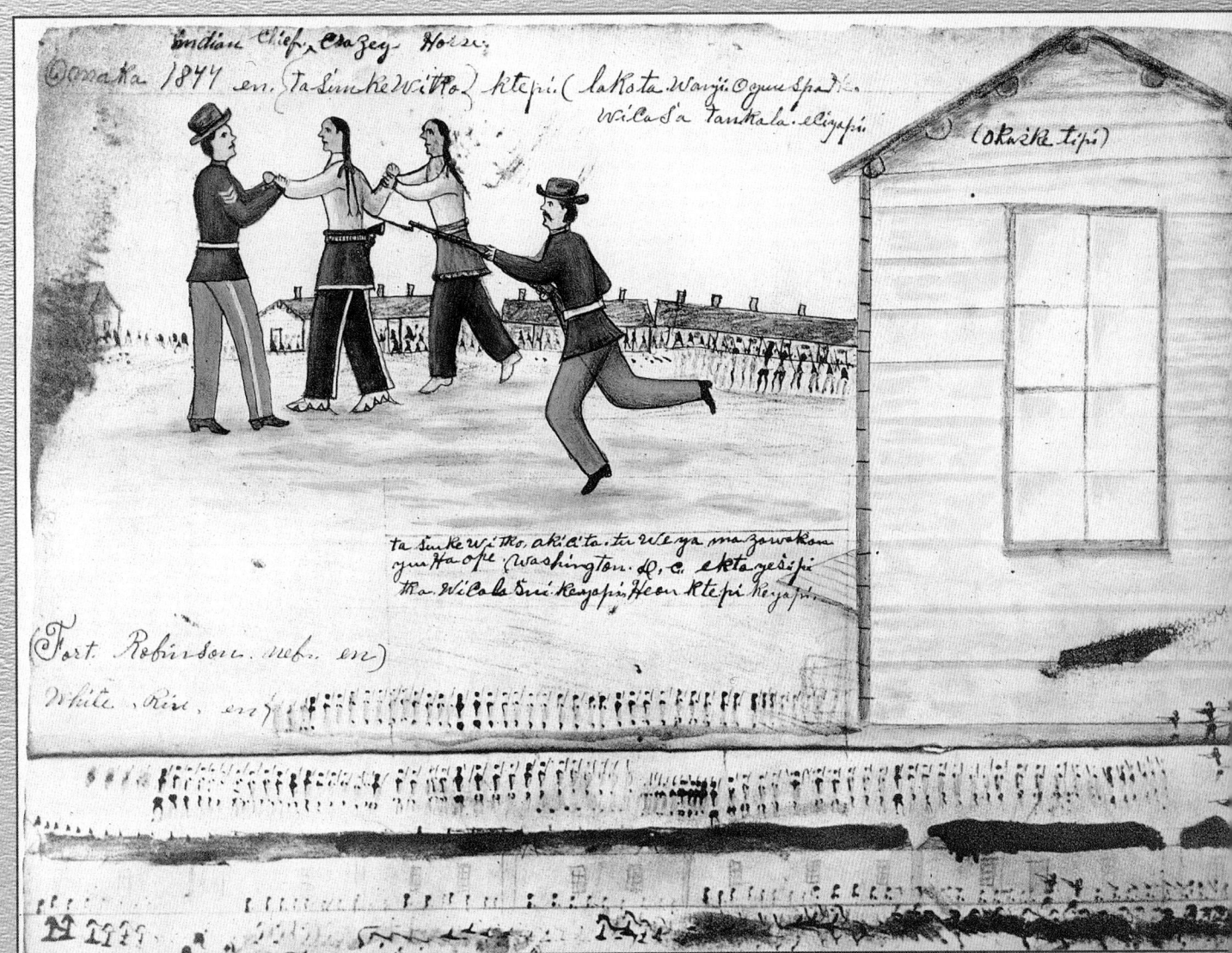

A Native American artist, Amos Bad Heart Buffalo, made this painting of the death of Crazy Horse. Amos Bad Heart Buffalo lived from 1869 to 1918.

The Man Remembered

Crazy Horse became a legend in history because of his daring exploits in battle. He was always the first to charge the enemy. He inspired bravery among his people and earned the respect of his enemies.

But he also became a legend among his own people for his charity, his humbleness, and his devotion to caring for the poor. He tried to live up to the ideals in his vision quest.

He was a complex man. All his life he preferred to be a loner. He failed to live up to the ideals of a Shirt-Wearer. He did not participate in treaty councils, and he even avoided the ceremonies of his own people. Crazy Horse preferred the solitude of the buffalo prairies.

This memorial to Crazy Horse was erected on the spot where he was killed. His burial site is unknown.

Thunderhead Mountain

Some day, the largest statue in the world will be a sculpture of Crazy Horse carved out of an entire mountain near Custer, South Dakota. For the last 50 years, sculptor Korczak Kiolkonski and his wife and children have been creating the carving, blasting it out of the mountain with explosives. It will be many years before the gigantic project is finished.

But whenever his people needed his war skills, he was a great military leader. His charity was even greater and made him truly beloved among his people. He remains a symbol of the continuing struggle of Native Americans for freedom, self-determination, and dignity.

Timeline

about **1838**–Crazy Horse born near Black Hills in present-day South Dakota.

1854–Dispute over cow leads to the deaths of Conquering Bear, Lieutenant Grattan, and 30 soldiers.

1855–U.S. Army retaliates by destroying Sincongu village at Bluewater Creek.

about **1856**–Crazy Horse goes on vision quest.
Crazy Horse earns his name.

1866–Crazy Horse helps Red Cloud defeat Captain Fetterman near Fort Phil Kearny.

1868–Treaty of Fort Laramie.

1874–Colonel Custer discovers gold in illegal expedition into Black Hills.

June 17, 1876–Battle of the Rosebud.

June 25, 1876–Battle of the Greasy Grass (Custer's Last Stand).

May 6, 1877–Crazy Horse surrenders.

Sept. 5, 1877–Crazy Horse is killed.

GLOSSARY

Agency (AY-juhn-see) The U.S. organization responsible for carrying out treaty obligations to a Native American tribe, such as providing food, education, and agricultural tools. The Indian agent was usually located at a U.S. Army post near the tribe's reservation.

Exterminate (ek-STUR-muh-nate) To kill all of the members of one species.

Gold rush (GOHLD RUHSH) A frantic rush of people to get to a new gold field.

Medicine man (MED-uh-suhn MAN) A religious leader who conducts ceremonies interprets dreams, and aids in healing.

Purification rituals (PYOOR-uh-fuh-kay-shuhn rich-OO-uhlz) Ceremonies that young Lakota men undertake under the guidance of a medicine man before going on a vision quest.

Raid (RAYD) A way for young warriors to prove themselves by stealing horses from other tribes.

Reservation (rez-ur-VAY-shun) Land that is reserved for Native American tribes. Indians were forced to leave their traditional homelands and settle on reservations.

Self-determination (SELF-di-tur-min-ay-shun) Deciding one's own future.

Tepees (TEE-peez) Indian tents made of poles and buffalo hides.

Treaty (TREE-tee) An agreement between two nations.

Tribal councils (TRY-buhl KOUN-suhl) Meetings of the chiefs and headmen to discuss issues facing the tribe.

Vision quest (VIZH-uhn KWEST) A search for a vision that gives guidance for how a young Lakota warrior should live his life, achieved through fasting, prayer, and solitude.

FURTHER READING AND INFORMATION

Books to Read

Bruchac, Joseph. *Crazy Horse's Vision*. New York: Lee & Low Books Inc., 2000.

Kotzwinkle, William. *The Return of Crazy Horse*. Berkeley, CA: North Atlantic Books, 2001.

Mavis, B. *Crazy Horse: Legends of the West*. Broomall, PA: Chelsea House Publishers, 1997.

Pownall, David. *Dream of Chief Crazy Horse*. New York: Theatre Communications Group Inc., 2001.

Videos

Biography—Crazy Horse. A&E Entertainment, 2000.

Crazy Horse. Turner Home Entertainment, 1996.

Crazy Horse and Custer. Front Row Video Inc., 2001.

INDEX

Amos Bad Heart Buffalo 27
Arapahos 12

Battles
    Little Bighorn, or Greasy Grass 5, *22*, 22-23, *23*
    Rosebud 20-21
Black Buffalo Woman 16
Black Hills (Paha Sapa) 6, 11, *11*, 15, 18, 19
Blue Water Creek massacre 9, 10
Bourke, Captain John G. 19
Bozeman Trail 12-13, 15, 20
buffalo 6, *6*, 8, 16, 17, 24, 25, 26
    overhunting 16-17, *17*, 25

Cheyenne 4, 20, 23, 24
Clark, Lieutenant (White Hat) 25
Conquering Bear 9
Crazy Horse 5, *12*
    childhood 6-7
    death 27, *27*, 28
    shirt-wearer 16-17, 28
    surrender 25
    vision quest 10-11, 12, 28
Crook, General George 21, *21*
Crow 23
Custer, Lieutenant Colonel George Armstrong 5, *5*, 18, *18*, 21, 22-23, *23*, 24

Deadwood 19

Fetterman massacre 14
Forts
    C. F. Smith 12
    Laramie 15
    Phil Kearny 12, 14, *14*, 15
    Reno 12, 15
    Robinson 25, *25*, 26, 27

Gall 23
gold rush 18-19, *19*
Grattan massacre 8-9

Great Plains 6, 9, 17

He Dog 10, 15, 25
Hinman, Eleanor 4, 10, 13, 15, 21, 22, 25
horses 7
Hump 23

Kills Two 5
Kiolkonski, Korczak 29

Lakotas 4, 6, 7, 10, 11, 12, 14, 16, 17, 18, 19, 20, 23, 24, 25
    Hunkpapa 7, 24
    Miniconju 7, 8-9
    Oglala 6, 7, 12-13, 15, 17, 24
    Sincongu 7, 8-9
Little Bighorn River, or Greasy Grass River 20, 21

No Water 16

Oregon Trail 8, *8*

railroad 16, *16*
Rattle Blanket Woman 7
Red Cloud 13, *13*, 15, 25
Red Horse 22
Reno, Miles 23
reservations 18-19, 26
Ricker, Judge E.S. 13

Sandoz, Mari 13
Sherman, General William Tecumseh 15, 26, *26*
Short Buffalo 4, 21, 22, 25
Sioux 7, 9, 10, 13, 15, 21
Sitting Bull 18, 19, 23, 24, *24*
Sun Dance *11*

Thunderhead Mountain 29, *29*
Treaty of Fort Laramie 15, *15*, 18
Two Moon 23